FUR

A Trapper's Guide to the Modern Fur Market

By Jeremiah Wood

Hello and welcome! I'm Jeremiah Wood from TrappingToday.com. As a trapper and outdoor writer I've always had a passion for sharing information with others who enjoy the things I do.

When I started TrappingToday.com, my goal was to provide updated trapping-related news and information to fellow trappers, and help build the knowledge base of the trapping community. Over time, I found that there was a huge information gap in the trapping world: **fur prices**. I began posting more information on my blog about fur auction results and price reports, and traffic to the site grew exponentially. I began to notice the same questions surfacing time and time again.

"Where can I sell my furs?" "What are (*insert species here*) pelt prices in (*insert state here*)?" "How do I know whether I'm getting a good price for my fur?" It became obvious that many of these questions didn't have easy answers. They required a more comprehensive approach. That's when I decided it was time to put together a book to help fur harvesters better understand the market and ensure they are getting the best possible prices for their pelts.

I've done my best to compile information on where and how to sell your fur and how to determine a fair price. In the guide I take a broad approach to the idea of using all available knowledge to get the most value out of the furbearers you trap. I also provide resources for you to find up to date fur price information from the international fur auctions and state auctions. I truly hope it's useful. Feel free to provide feedback, suggestions and further questions to me at jrodwood@gmail.com. Enjoy!

TABLE OF CONTENTS

FUR MARKET OVERVIEW

Fur has value. It's the thing that separates trapping from most hunting and fishing pursuits. Not only does trapping provide recreational and cultural value, but it also results in the harvest of a fur pelt that has a financial value, and supports economies worldwide. That's one of the things that attracted me to trapping as a kid. The possibility of combining my love for the outdoors and animals with a chance to provide a paycheck and the freedom associated with it was like a dream come true. In reality the economic benefits were smaller than I'd hoped, but when combined with the other benefits I enjoy as a trapper, it's really tough to beat. It wasn't always that way, though, and the fur market once provided a good living for many rural Americans. Fur prices are much lower today, but a trapper who knows the market well and thinks creatively can still make it pay.

History of the Fur Market
The world fur market has a history that dates back hundreds of years. At least as early as the middle ages, Europeans imported raw furs from animals caught primarily in Russia to make hats, gloves and coats to stay warm. Over the years, the Russians expanded westward in search of valuable furbearers, first to Siberia, and then North America, particularly in western Alaska. Around the time that America was discovered and colonies were developing, demand for fur pelts in Europe was at an all time high.

 Furbearer populations in Europe were not adequate to satisfy the high market demand, particularly for beaver. Beaver fur was processed into felt, which was used to make highly fashionable hats. This resulted in the French and

English joining the Russians as the major players in the world fur market. The French developed the fur trade in large parts of Canada, while the English established trade in the American colonies, with some investment in Canadian fur trading via the Hudson's Bay Company. The high price of fur pelts encouraged the exploration of the New World and establishment of the fur trade in North America. At first, traders exchanged goods with indigenous peoples for fur pelts, but soon enterprising trappers began venturing into the vast unsettled territory in search of fur.

The high demand for fur played a primary role in the exploration and settlement of North America. Fur prices were high enough to provide incentive for vast expeditions into dangerous and unknown territory by adventurers and common folks alike. Fur was a valuable resource that provided a source of wealth great enough to spur the development of an entire continent. Over time, felt hats and other fur items fell out of fashion in Europe, and were replaced by other materials. The fur trade declined dramatically in both size and scope between the 19th century and today.

Modern Fur Market

Despite its declines from historic levels, the fur industry remains alive today. Modern wildlife management practices combined with a lower global demand for fur have resulted in overly abundant populations of many furbearers. These furbearers represent a valuable, renewable resource available at a relatively low price for the garment trade.

The demand for raw furs in the modern market is dominated by China and Russia. Unlike the United States, where wearing fur has fallen out of the mainstream, fur remains fashionable in these parts of the world. These two large countries are also experiencing significant economic growth in the middle class, with more buying power becoming available to more people every year. Fur is considered a status symbol to many, and a large part of this newfound economic wealth goes toward the purchase of fur.

In areas with colder climates such as Russia and parts of China, fur is also a utility item, used to keep warm just as much as it is for fashion. Colder winters in these areas thus increase the demand for fur.

Large-Scale Factors that Influence Fur Prices

Basic economic theory dictates that supply and demand work together to affect prices, and the fur market is no exception to this rule.

Supply

Fur is supplied from two main avenues: fur produced in farms/ranches, and fur caught by trappers in the wild. Ranched fur represents about 80% of all fur supplied in the world, and is mainly comprised of just two species: mink and fox. Supply of ranched fur is highly dependent on operating costs and fur prices, and can fluctuate substantially over time. In periods of high fur prices, fur farms increase their production to sell more pelts in the market. This increased supply, without a corresponding increase in demand, causes prices to drop. When prices drop low enough for fur farms to start losing money, they cut back on production, and some 'pelt out', or sell their entire inventory of furbearers, including breeding stock. This decreases the supply to a point where it can't keep up with demand, prices rise and the cycle starts over again.

Similarly, supply of wild fur depends on operating costs (fuel, traps, lure, bait, etc), and prices received for fur, but does not respond in direct correlation to these factors. This is mainly because very few trappers rely on fur as a sole source of income, and often fur is sold at or below the cost to trap it. Some trappers will slow or stop operations during times of low prices, but many continue to trap and supply the market during these low times. Supply of wild caught fur only responds substantially during periods of extremely low or extremely high prices.

Demand

Demand from the major fur consuming countries plays the greatest role in influencing prices. Because just a few countries purchase most of the fur, activities in those countries have a huge impact on the market. That's why warm winters in Russia and China (especially) always seem to put a damper on the fur market. Additionally, economic conditions can greatly influence the market. For instance, Russia's economy is severely dependent on oil revenue, so a substantial drop in crude oil prices tends to weaken Russian demand for fur, and result in lower prices. Factors that influence the Chinese economy can impact demand for fur as well. China's astounding rate of economic growth over the past couple of decades has seemingly stagnated. Fur items normally bought by China consequently have far less value than they did a few years ago. The Chinese government also imposes high tariffs on imported fur, and many Chinese fur buyers have found themselves in serious trouble the past few years for trying to avoid these taxes. Economic conditions in major fur buying countries are an important underlying source of demand for fur, and play a critical role in fur price levels.

Fashion Trends

In addition to factors that affect overall fur prices, fashion trends can impact markets for individual fur items, and cause their price to fluctuate wildly. By definition, a trend doesn't remain constant, and fashion doesn't have to make sense, it just happens to be what the right people think is 'in' at the time, and what they're willing to pay for. Fashion trends tend to impact prices of rare fur items more drastically than those that appear in the market in high volumes. For instance, pelts of lower quantity items like gray fox, otter and fisher have seen more drastic price fluctuations due to fashion trends than common furs like beaver and raccoon have.

Major Furs and Their Role in the Market

To understand how climatic and economic factors influence prices of particular fur items, it's important to know who tends to purchase what in the global fur market. Here's a brief overview, focusing on a few of the major furbearers.

Mink – Used primarily in the manufacture of fashionable coats, the majority of mink fur in the market comes from farms, often termed 'ranch mink'. Ranch mink pelts are commonly 2-3 times the size of wild mink, and they offer a quality and consistency that makes them much more marketable. Wild mink are always less valuable than ranch mink, and wild mink prices are often driven by the ranch market, meaning that high ranch mink prices will improve the price of wild mink. China purchases the vast majority of mink in the world fur market, followed by Russia at a distant second. China's fur farming industry has grown substantially in recent years, taking market share from ranch mink producers in other countries.

Raccoon – Russia dominates the market for raccoon pelts, and a poor Russian economy really puts a damper on the coon market. Articles made from raccoon and purchased by Russian consumers are typically worn by a large percentage of the middle class population, not only as a fashion item, but as a necessity to keep warm. When the Russian economy suffers, the middle class struggles to put food on the table and has little to no extra funds to spend on fur hats and coats.

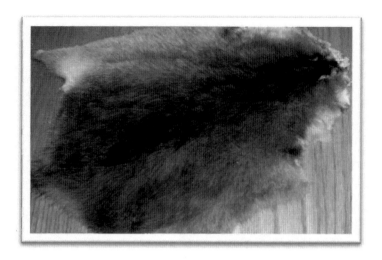

Muskrat - China is the major buyer of muskrat in the market, but not the end consumer. The Chinese purchase and process the muskrat skins, most of which end up on store shelves in Korea. Muskrat bellies are often used as liners for men's coats, and the backs are used in other items such as accessories. The Korean government has placed heavy taxes on fur garments in the past, but has recently lifted these taxes, meaning the market should fare better relative to most other items.

Beaver - The market for beaver pelts has been perhaps one of the most disappointing aspects of the overall fur trade in the modern era. Beaver are plentiful and relatively easy to trap, but require a lot of work to skin, flesh and stretch. From a buyer's perspective, it would seem that beaver pelts offer a lot of volume for the price. The trouble is that it costs a lot of money to dress a beaver pelt in preparation for use in fur garments. Beaver competes directly with mink for use in garments, and the higher dressing cost, along with low mink prices continue to depress the beaver market. Historically, trappers made a lot of money on beaver, but it would seem that those days are over for now.

Otter - Pelts from otters offer the highest density and durability of all furs. Still, low demand for mink and beaver typically impact otter prices. Several years back, otter was a hot fashion item and commanded very high prices, but that trend has passed, and otter typically stays in line with most other items today. China seems to be the main buyer.

Bobcat - Recently, bobcats have produced serious money for western trappers. Top quality cats with thick fur and wide, white spotted bellies have been a huge fashion item of late. Russia has been the main player in this market, and a weak Russian economy can hurt cat prices some. However, high quality spotted bobcats are only available in small quantities, and they are part of a high end specialty market, supported by buyers with lots of disposable income even in tough economic times.

<u>Coyote</u> – Furs of coyote are primarily used as trim for down-filled coats. This market is strong in the United States and Europe, and coyote should continue to do well in the near future as a result.

Marten and Fisher - A variety of countries purchase marten for the fur trade, but Korea plays a large and growing part of this market. Favorable tax cuts will help the Korean market and marten should do well. Fisher has always been a relatively valuable fur item, but has fluctuated over time, and male and female furs vary considerably in their makeup, and price. Male fishers tend to have coarser fur, while female furs are soft and silky.

Currently, the fashion market is favoring female fishers in China, where they are used as trim on mink coats, while the males are mainly purchased by Russia. The fashion trend is allowing for high prices on females and small, silky males, but most male fishers will see lower prices with a poor Russian economy.

Review

As you can see, the modern fur market is an incredibly complex thing. Conditions can change in a hurry, and fur prices can fluctuate substantially based on worldwide economic factors. That's why you need up to date information in order to understand the latest market news and how it affects how you sell your fur. At TrappingToday.com I provide fur price updates, news and related articles to keep you informed. In addition, North American Fur Auctions is a great resource to stay on top of market conditions. The folks at NAFA are connected to the global fur market and constantly have their fingers on the pulse. Similarly, Fur Harvesters Auction markets much of the wild fur produced in North America, and are another source for fur market information. Remember not to believe everything you hear from auction companies, though. It's their job to convince you to market fur through them, and their reports can sometimes be a little overly optimistic.

HOW TO SELL YOUR FUR

Let's say you're a new trapper looking for the best way to sell your fur. Or perhaps you are an experienced hand who is looking for an alternative selling method that might better suit your needs or provide more profit. Here, we take a look at the different fur selling options and discuss the pros and cons of each.

From Harvest to Garment
In the fur market, the same single fur product can be sold in a number of different forms, from the whole, harvested animal to a completed fur garment, and any stage in between. We'll talk in detail about the major options below, but first let's go through an overview of the process.

1) Harvest – furbearing animal is harvested from the wild
2) Skinning – skin/hide is removed from the animal
3) Fleshing – fat and flesh is scraped from the hide to keep it from spoiling
4) Stretching – hide is stretched, typically on a wire or board, to give it proper shape in drying
5) Drying – hide is dried and placed in a cool, dark environment for short term storage
6) Tanning – through a chemical and mechanical process, fur is tanned for long term preservation
7) Garment Making – tanned fur is cut and sewn into garments in the manufacture of fur coats, hats, gloves, trim and specialty items.

Most of the fur purchased from trappers is termed 'raw fur', which is fur that has been skinned, fleshed, stretched and dried. However, you can sell fur at a number of different stages, depending on market conditions and your individual preferences and needs.

Carcass Fur

Selling fur on the carcass (often termed 'in the round') is a nice option for a part time hobby fur taker or inexperienced harvester who doesn't want to learn how to properly skin, flesh, stretch and dry fur. Sometimes it seems there is hardly enough time to go trapping or hunting, and investing all of that extra time into prepping fur isn't feasible. This is the simplest form of selling fur, where you harvest the animal and bring it directly to the fur buyer. The buyer then skins it and prepares it for further stages of the production chain.

Advantages to selling fur in the round are that you can save a lot of time, and don't risk lowering the quality of the fur by making mistakes during processing. The main disadvantages, however, are finding a buyer and taking a much lower price. It's very difficult nowadays to find a buyer for carcass fur. Whole carcasses are prone to spoilage and can't be shipped, meaning they have to be sold locally, and the number of country fur buyers willing to buy carcass fur has declined over the years.

You'll have to accept a much lower price for carcass fur because of the considerable time and effort it takes to prepare fur. The cost of preparation relative to overall value of fur is at an all time high, meaning you'll find it pretty difficult to make a profit selling fur on the carcass.
In addition, many trappers look down on the practice of selling carcass fur because properly preparing fur is considered an art, and an important part of the trapping heritage. For most, taking the fur to the stretched, dried product is a critical part of the fur harvesting process.

Another option is to hire an experienced fur handler to skin and prep your fur for you market, but usually that isn't feasible except for with high value items.

Green Fur

Green fur refers to a fur pelt that has been skinned from the animal, but has not yet been fleshed, stretched and dried. The advantage to green fur is that animals can be skinned and the green pelt stored in the short-term or sold without having to lug carcasses around.

Selling green fur saves the buyer some skinning time, and they are able to flesh, stretch and dry the pelts in a uniform manner. However, not all buyers purchase green fur, and you'll still get a lower price because of the extra effort the buyer has to go through to prepare the fur. This can be a good option for folks who harvest a large amount of critters and don't want to prepare all of their own fur, but only see a buyer periodically. Traveling regional fur buyers like Groenewold Fur & Wool Company buy large quantities of green fur.

Raw Fur

The vast majority of fur sold by trappers is raw fur, which has been skinned, fleshed, stretched and dried. Raw fur does have a shelf life, but can be stored in a cool, dry place for a few months. It can also be frozen for long term storage. Because it can be packed tightly and is light and flexible, raw fur can be shipped cost effectively in large quantities.

Much of the raw fur sold to country buyers ends up being shipped to large auction houses, the majority being sold to major entities that tan and prepare it for garment making. A lot goes into properly preparing fur to get the maximum value from each pelt, and the methods vary for each species. Raw fur sells at significantly higher prices compared to green and carcass fur. You can find resources on fur preparation at TrappingToday.com.

Tanned Fur

As a trapper or fur hunter wanting to tan your fur to sell, keep in mind that fur buyers purchase very little tanned fur, so selling tanned fur requires a specialized marketing strategy. You can tan fur on your own, but it is a long, difficult and labor intensive process. Another option is to send fur to be tanned at a tannery. Several tanneries specialize in tanning fur for trappers, and we'll discuss them a little later on in this book.

Finished Fur Product

A final option for selling your fur is taking it all the way to a final, finished product. There are some specialty markets for fur products, but they are small and often easily saturated. Still, when fur prices are low, selling fur hats, gloves and other items can be quite profitable. We'll discuss more later on.

WHERE TO SELL YOUR FUR

Regardless of whether you're new or experienced, a weekend warrior or long-line fur trapper, it's important to find the best market for your fur. In some areas, it can even be difficult to find any place to sell your fur at all. Fur markets exist for trappers everywhere, though, and we'll explore the different markets here.

In this section, we'll explore all of the different avenues to sell your fur, from the local country fur buyer to the international auction houses. In addition, we'll discuss a couple of alternatives you can explore, and with some extra time and effort, add a great deal of value to your fur.

Country Fur Buyers

Many a trapper owes a debt of gratitude to the country fur buyer. Throughout the generations, these buyers have shared local trapping knowledge and fur preparation advice, and have been the connection between local trappers and the complex international fur market. The country buyer is most often a local in the community, an old timer with lots of wisdom to offer, a trapper (or former trapper), and just a plain old honest, fair person to deal with.

You won't be paid the highest prices because the country buyer is purchasing fur in small quantities, and much of that fur will go to one of the auction houses that any trapper can send their fur to. The country buyer will typically pay cash, and buy during the trapping season when there is still a lot of uncertainty in the market. He's taking a big risk with his money, and regardless of the outcome, won't be making a fortune even if fur prices rise.

Country buyers often will purchase fur 'in the round', or on the carcass. This is convenient for folks who don't want to prepare their own fur. In recent years, however, it's gotten more difficult to find buyers willing to do this.

The greatest advantages of selling fur to the local buyer have little to do with money, although it's nice to get quick cash when you have bills to pay. The local fur buyer provides knowledge that money often can't buy. Most of what I learned about handling fur came from local buyers. Their feedback on what you did right and did wrong can be well worth the difference in price you might receive for selling your fur locally.

One of the problems with local fur buyers is that they are becoming increasingly hard to find. Most of the buyers are throwbacks from the fur boom days, and the poor fur market and overall aging of today's trapping community means that there are fewer of them around. There isn't much, if any, profit to be made, so these guys are doing the work for the love, not the money. As the old timers pass away, they often aren't replaced. If you have a good local fur buyer in your area, I highly recommend working with them. If not, you'll have to explore the other options listed below.

Regional Fur Buyers

The next step up from country fur buyer is the regional buyer. These buyers operate on a larger scale than the typical country buyer. Because they handle more fur, they often have the quantities needed to deal directly with big players in the international fur market, meaning they have orders to fill, often at pre-arranged prices. They have more money to work with, and can often pay more for your fur. They can't always pay top prices, however, because they deal in an industry with high risk, and their business model requires consistent profits to survive.

There are two ways to sell fur to regional buyers: ship it, or meet them at a pickup route. Shipping your fur directly to the buyer is convenient, as you can do it any time and the cost is quite reasonable. However, the disadvantage is that you won't get a price until they are able to look at the fur in person. They then make you an offer and you either accept, or have them ship the fur back to you. The shipping cost and time tied up in the selling process can make this type of sales model a difficult one.

Many regional buyers have pickup routes throughout a large region, meaning you can often meet a buyer in a nearby location to sell your fur. They can look at your fur and offer a price, and you have the option to take the money or keep your fur, without the shipping cost. However, routes are only run so often and may not always work well with your schedule.

Groenewold Fur & Wool Company is the largest of what I would consider regional fur buyers. They operate out of Illinois, and run fur routes in many different states in the upper Midwest and the Southeast. For those states, you can follow their route schedule and meet a buyer when they swing through a town near you. They buy fur in the round, green, or raw. If you don't live in one of those states, you can ship raw fur to their Illinois address. Groenewold offers fur market updates and advice for fur harvesting and pelt preparation from a buyer's perspective. They are a well established, reputable company with a long and successful history in the fur trade. You can find them at www.gfwco.com.

Petska Fur is a Nebraska company that purchases fur along routes in 11 western states, and takes fur by mail as well. They purchase fur in the round, green and finished raw fur as well. See www.petskafur.com for more information.

KanOkla Fur Company is based in South Haven, Kansas, and buys fur along scheduled pickup routes throughout Kansas and Oklahoma. They also buy fur in the round, green or raw. Find them at www.kanoklafurco.com.

Those are some of the major regional fur buyers, though there are several others, and some come and go from year to year depending on the strength of the market. If you need money fast, and one of these buyers runs a route in your area, the regional fur buyer can provide a great opportunity for you to sell your fur.

State Auctions
Almost every state in the U.S., as well as each Canadian province, has its own trappers association. Trappers associations are extremely important because they effectively provide trappers with a strong, united voice to protect trapping rights and traditions in the face of legal challenges from animal rights groups. Associations also provide a place for trappers to gather, share ideas, exchange goods, and just plain help keep the trapping community alive. I strongly encourage you to join and become active in your trappers association.

Another benefit of trappers associations is that many hold annual fur auctions, allowing trappers to gather together with large quantities of fur and hopefully attract buyers and increase prices paid for furs. Buyers who attend trappers association auctions are often small country buyers or regional fur companies, who then sell to foreign interests or send the fur to the larger auctions. The price advantage of the state auction is that several buyers are competing for fur, meaning that during a high market, prices can be quite good. These auctions will almost never command the top prices, though, because there usually isn't enough fur present to attract the biggest buyers.

In my experience, the trappers association auction provides an excellent balance between the sharing of local knowledge and getting a decent price for fur. Fur sale commissions typically go to the association, and are then used, in most cases, to promote and/or protect trapping on the state level. And the state auctions can be a lot of fun, to boot!

If you're not aware of your area trappers association or the fur auctions it sponsors, you can visit www.trappingtoday.com/state-trappers-asssociations/ to find yours. I often provide reports of average prices from these auctions at trappingtoday.com.

International Auction Houses

The majority of the fur produced in North America goes through two major auction houses, **North American Fur Auctions** and **Fur Harvesters Auction**. Whether it's purchased by a local fur buyer or sent by individual trappers, these two auction houses sell huge volumes of fur at some of the best prices to the top buyers in the world fur market.

Anyone can send fur to the major auction houses, and many trappers choose this route because they typically provide the best opportunity to maximize value from their fur. While one obvious advantage to using these services is price, another is the fact that in most cases, your fur will sell and you will be paid, even if the price is low (in poor market years this hasn't always been the case). Another advantage is that these auction houses spend a great deal of time and money promoting wild fur on the world fashion scene, and do a great job creating and optimizing markets for fur.

The disadvantages of sending fur to the big auction houses are real as well. First, only raw fur is accepted at these auctions. This means you will have to skin, flesh, stretch and dry all of your fur to send to them. Second, you have to send fur well in advance of the auctions dates. Third, you often wait several months to get paid. Finally, the price you'll get for you fur is unknown at the time you ship it, meaning that you're at the mercy of the market.

If the market is very poor, large quantities of fur can be held back by the auction house in anticipation of a better sale later on, which means it can sometimes take a couple of years to get paid. There is a level of risk involved in this model. Still, it's a great way to sell fur and during good times, provides some of the maximum profits available for trappers. Let's dig into some detail on NAFA and FHA.

North American Fur Auctions (NAFA)

North American Fur Auctions is the largest fur auction house in North America, and the second largest in the world. NAFA sells fur both from fur farmers (mostly ranch mink and some fox) and wild fur harvested from trappers. NAFA is based in Ontario, Canada, and has offices in Manitoba, Wisconsin and Holland.

NAFA holds several wild fur auctions each year. Wild fur and ranch fur auctions are held separately, but often back-to-back, and the ranch fur auctions are typically held first. Ranch fur prices often provide a valuable gauge to predict wild fur prices. Due to the large volume of fur offered, NAFA's auctions attract buyers from all over the world, mostly from the major fur buying areas of Russia, China, Korea and parts of Europe.

NAFA's auction process is pretty neat, and you can now watch it live online. They post auction results and prices by species promptly after auction completion as well. Each person who ships fur to NAFA can log onto an online account and see the status of their fur items – how the fur graded, whether it sold, and what the sale price was.

During difficult market times, NAFA reserves the right to refuse to sell certain fur items they think are not receiving the price they should, meaning that trappers don't always end up eating the cost of a poor auction turnout. In addition to the auction, NAFA offers private treaty sales on furs that don't sell at auction, simply because fur does not have an indefinite shelf life, and must eventually be sold, even if at a very low price.

Selling Your Fur Through NAFA
Anyone can sell fur through NAFA, and the company makes it pretty easy to do so. On their website, www.nafa.ca, they provide information on the auction dates and last receiving dates. Last receiving date is basically the deadline at which you need to get your fur to NAFA for it to show up in the next auction. You can send fur to NAFA any time. If you miss the last receiving date for a specific auction, your fur will be held for the following auction.

NAFA offers a great deal of options for getting your fur to them. They have a network of fur receiving depots throughout the country, with a primary focus on areas that don't have a lot of fur buyers available and have lots of trappers who ship them quality fur. They have pickup routes where you can deliver your fur. If you are not in an area with an established depot or route, you can simply ship your fur to their Stoughton, WI office. I've done it before and the process was simple. You can find more about shipping to NAFA on their website.

Though NAFA offers some of the best fur prices, the commissions are quite high. For regular shippers, the commission payment is 11%. This is taken out of your account prior to NAFA cutting you a check. If you haven't shipped to NAFA before, they create an account for you when they get your fur. You have the option of joining what they call the "Wild Fur Shippers Council". WSFC membership costs $25 a year, and your commission payments drop to 9%. You also save money on fur shipping costs. If you ship a large volume of fur (more than $1,000 worth), membership in WFSC can pay for itself quickly.

Overall, NAFA is a great place to sell fur if you can put up high quality raw fur and don't mind taking some risk and waiting to get paid. You can send fur from anywhere in the country and know you'll have access to some of the best fur prices the market can offer.

Fur Harvesters Auction (FHA)

Fur Harvesters Auction is also located in Ontario, and operates extremely similar to NAFA. The company is smaller than NAFA and focuses more on wild fur and less on ranched fur, but for the most part offers the exact same advantages and disadvantages of NAFA.

Anyone can send their fur to FHA to be auctioned off. If you live in Canada you can ship directly to FHA, but if you live in the U.S. you'll have to ship it to one of their receiving depots on this side of the border to avoid complications with customs. Similar to NAFA, you can drop your fur off with an agent on a pick-up route, or at a depot. You can find more details and a list of agents and depots at www.furharvesters.com.

FHA auctions usually take place in Ontario, but recently they've started holding one of their sales in Helsinki, Finland in conjunction with ranch fur sales. This has allowed them to attract more buyers and has resulted in better prices, making it possibly the best major fur sale of the season in recent years.

NAFA vs. FHA
Trappers have long debated which of the two major auction houses is a better place to sell fur. Each has its advantages and disadvantages, but at the end of the day, the two companies operate so similarly, that it's probably a toss-up. Having both companies around is a great advantage to fur sellers, because competition between the two keeps them on their toes.

If you put up good fur, can wait a few months for a check, and don't mind paying a commission, the major fur auction houses can be a great place to get the most value for your fur.

Overview
As you can see, there are a variety of options to consider when selling your fur. Remember that you don't have to choose just one. A smart trapper often hedges their bets, selling fur to a variety of sources to learn what works best for them. Remember, each fur sale is a learning experience, and you can use the knowledge you gain to maximize fur revenue in future seasons.

UNDERSTANDING FUR PRICES

Fur prices are at the top of most every trapper's mind. There's a huge demand for information on fur prices, and that's partly because prices can be difficult to predict, especially during uncertain times in the fur market.

It is difficult to communicate fur prices in simple numbers because those numbers can change drastically over time, and also depend greatly on the quality of the fur you're selling and the region it comes from. I developed this guide for fur harvesters who want to stay on top of the fur market and understand how to get the most value from their fur.

I publish fur market forecasts and fur price reports regularly on Trapping Today, but many trappers are still confused about how these numbers apply to the furs they trap. That's why it's important that you as a trapper have a basic understanding of how to take fur price reports and apply them to your specific situation and the furs you have to sell. In the following pages we'll discuss the different variables that impact the quality and price paid for fur, and help you get an idea of what the fur you trap is worth relative to the overall market.

Seasonal Variation in Fur Quality

An animal's fur coat undergoes significant changes throughout the course of the year to deal with different climates, and the market demands pelts that have full, thick fur in prime condition. This prime pelt condition coincides with the winter months, and many state and provincial regulations set trapping seasons to coincide with fur primeness to ensure maximum value of harvested animals. Still, every year there are trappers who harvest animals early in the season before the fur is prime, and get a poor price. This is common with raccoon, which are easier to harvest early in the season before freeze-up, and whose fur tends to prime a bit later than that. The term 'blue coon' refers to a raccoon pelt that hasn't yet reached its prime, and has a dark, bluish appearance when the hide is turned out and dried. A fully prime fur will have a distinctly light colored hide, and the difference between blue and white can be as little as a couple of weeks' time.

To get the maximum value for your fur, be sure to trap it during its peak primeness whenever possible. If that's not feasible, then realize that you'll get less value for those unprime pelts. In years of high fur demand, unprime pelts may not see a huge price break because buyers are willing to be less choosy when they have orders to fill. When demand is low and fur supply is high, though, sometimes it can be impossible to even sell these unprime pelts, and if sold, they are often worth just a fraction of the price of prime fur.

While fur quality varies significantly between northern and southern regions, the timing of primeness varies less, and coincides with the shortest months of the year. In areas of the deep southern U.S., some furs never get prime and don't hold much more value in winter than they do in summer.

Fur Primeness Charts

Fur primeness for a particular species varies by area, and many states and provinces have their own version of a fur primeness chart – a graph showing when fur is thick and full enough to have trapping value, and the period of peak primeness.

In general, most species in most areas begin to prime up in November, and remain prime until sometime in January or February. Coyote and fox tend to prime up earlier, and beaver and muskrats stay prime much later than most other species. Again, this varies a lot. Most trapping seasons line up well with fur primeness. Again, you may not be able to trap effectively during times of peak fur primeness, meaning much of your fur may be under or over prime. Just understand that means you'll average less per pelt, and in some years, the fur may be tough to sell.

Regional Variation in Fur Quality

Fur pelts are valued primarily based on their usefulness in the garment market. That means that thick, full, prime northern fur has a much higher value than flat, dull southern fur. Furbearers have coats that are adapted to their environment, meaning that individuals of the same species will develop very different fur coats based on the climate they live in. A red fox in Montana will have a much thicker coat than one in Louisiana, and the value of the pelt will be reflected in that. That's why southern fur almost always sells for less money than northern fur. You must take this into account when looking at fur price forecasts and reports.

In addition to the general pattern of better, thicker fur in northern climates, there are other factors that make fur more valuable in some regions than others. The greatest example of this is with bobcats. Bobcat fur value varies significantly among regions of North America, with western 'cats selling for far better prices than southern or eastern 'cats. The best bobcat pelts come from the American West, in states like Idaho, Montana, Colorado, Utah and Nevada. A few years back, these bobcats were selling for incredibly high averages of $500-$1,000 apiece!

Not only do the high desert bobcats have thick fur to withstand harsh winters, they have unique white, spotted bellies that make absolutely beautiful furs. Southern spotted 'cats don't have the fur thickness, and northeastern 'cats don't have the spotted bellies. Bobcats from these regions rarely average more than $50-$100 each.

Coyotes are another example of a fur item that experiences large regional differences in fur value. Fur thickness and quality change significantly between north and south, and in the northern latitudes, there is a huge east-west difference in prices. Western coyotes can be three times as valuable as their eastern counterparts because they have a uniform, pale coloration that makes them desirable as a trim item on down fur coats. They also have a thicker, softer fur than eastern coyotes, which often have long coarse hair similar to a German shepherd.

Not all species change significantly in value based on area. Mink and otter prices seem to be fairly consistent regardless of region. Muskrat and beaver don't change much in value except that there is significantly more demand for the thicker, northern pelts as a general rule. The hatter (felt) market for beaver doesn't require prime pelts, so southern beavers average much closer to northern beavers when that market is strong.

Fashion Trends

By definition, a trend is something that doesn't remain constant. Fashion trends come and go, and can greatly impact the value of certain fur items. It was the trend of the beaver felt hat in Europe that led to the huge demand for fur and the pioneering of the fur trade in North America. When that trend changed and beaver hats went out of style, the market crashed.

In the domestic animal market, Australian sheep skin boots, or uggs, became a major fashion trend in the U.S., and were the primary reason for an increase in sheep skin prices by up to 80% between 2010 and 2012. A Chinese trend in fur-lined ladies boots propped up the raccoon market several years back, and other items like gray fox and bobcat have experienced major price shifts due to fashion trends. A boost in demand for certain fur items due to a fashion trend can be a great bonus, but remember that these trends almost never last long, and can't be relied on over the long term.

True market value
When seeking the price of a certain fur pelt, keep in mind that no one can accurately predict or report such prices with absolute certainty. There is no fixed price on a certain pelt for a certain area. Price is determined through a mutual agreement between a buyer and a seller. A fair auction with a large number of buyers is probably the truest discovery of price available in today's market. Prices established in other sale agreements, whether at local auctions or dealings with local or regional buyers, will be influenced by the large auctions, but may vary widely depending on circumstances.

Given all of the factors influencing prices for particular types of fur, it's then important to understand where the fur you trap falls within the overall market. For instance, if you trap coyotes in Montana or bobcats in Nevada, you can expect to consistently average near the top of those markets each year. If you trap marten in Montana, though, your pelts will be on the low end of the marten averages. Maine beaver will be near the top, while Alaska will dominate in marten prices.

Other than asking other experienced trappers, there are two great ways to learn how your fur should do in the overall market: 1. Check your state auction results (they will almost always reflect prices for local fur). 2. Send a bunch of your fur to an international auction, and see where it grades in relation to the rest of the fur for that species. Understanding the basis for the fur you trap (what prices you get compared to the overall market) is critical to properly interpreting fur auction results and price reports.

ALTERNATIVES TO SELLING RAW FUR

As a general rule, trappers sell raw fur, skinned, stretched and dried. The international buyers are the end of the raw fur production line, and they have massive quantities of fur tanned and prepared for garment making.

Sometimes, however, trappers can find good profit opportunities by thinking outside the box. Instead of selling raw fur, you can sell tanned fur or sell finished fur garments. Now to be honest, the demand for these specialty items is relatively small. But if you're looking at a very poor price for raw fur, specialty markets can pay off.

Tanned Fur

Folks buy tanned fur pelts to decorate their homes and cabins. Some will buy tanned fur to turn it into articles of clothing or other decorative items. Anglers who tie fishing flies will buy patches of fur to tie with. Numerous other uses exist for fur items, but remember that they are specialty uses and the market can change based on supply and demand, disposable income and fads and trends.

To sell tanned fur, you obviously need to get it tanned. Tanning kills bacteria, preserves the skin and provides a soft, supple finish that lasts indefinitely – in other words, tanned fur is clean, safe and doesn't spoil. So how do you get your furs tanned?

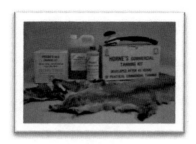

DIY Tanning
Self-tanning is one option. Tanning kits can be purchased online or at taxidermy supply or sporting goods stores. The most basic kits include the ingredients you need to tan about 20 lbs of wet skin weight for around $30-40. In addition, you'll probably need a few basic ingredients from the grocery store, a container or two to hold enough water to cover the hides and ingredients, and a whole lot of time and patience. If you don't mind the extra work, this might be a good option to explore. Be prepared for a huge learning curve and the possibility that your hides won't turn out perfect the first few times.

Custom Tanning

Moyle Mink & Tannery

Instead of tanning your own fur, you can send it to a tannery. While the old days of a tannery in every northeast river town are long gone, there are a few tanning operations around that cater to individual trappers. Moyle Mink & Tannery in Heyburn, Idaho is the most well known and established outfit around. They will tan individual furs in small quantities, but it's expensive. For instance, it currently costs $13.50 to tan a muskrat, but the price tiers down as quantity tanned increases, and if you send more than 20 'rats, the cost is $6.75 apiece, and more than 100 can be tanned for $5.50 each. These pricing tiers are significant because $5-6 can mean the difference between profit and loss. Larger skins like fox and coyotes will cost around $20-30 each.

Nearby in Rupert, Idaho, Furs For Fun is a smaller, but very similar tanning operation. Their prices are similar as well. Several other outfits tan fur at similar prices, including USA Foxx, which we'll discuss below. I have had fur tanned by both Moyle and Furs For Fun, which is run by a former Moyle employee. I've been satisfied with product from both operations. The only tough part about this type of tanning is the long waiting period to get your tanned furs. If I remember right, it's usually about a 2-3 month process, depending on time of year. Sometimes it takes up to six months. In most cases, you can pay more for faster service.

In some regions, local tanneries operate on a small scale, and may be an even better option to get furs tanned quickly and affordably. Ask your local taxidermist. They'll know of any tannery services available in the area.

To justify the extra time, money and effort invested in tanning your fur for sale, you obviously have to sell it at a price substantially higher than raw fur value. Several options exist. You can sell tanned fur online, primarily through Ebay or Etsy, and in some cases through other media channels like Facebook, Instagram, and even your own website. You can also consign fur through local gift shops, convenience stores, sporting goods stores, craft fairs and various other local outlets.

Selling tanned fur online via Ebay has a lot of advantages. With a little time and effort, anyone can do it, and folks from all over the country, and even throughout the world, can purchase your fur. You can sell at a set price, or sell the fur in an online auction and take some risk for higher potential reward. However, the advantage of this being such an easy process can also be a drawback, because dozens of other trappers are also selling their pelts on Ebay, and more supply relative to demand brings the market down. So this option usually comes with pretty thin margins.

Let's look at a couple of examples of selling tanned fur through Ebay.com. First let's pretend we're looking to sell muskrats. Let's say the going price for muskrat raw fur is around $3/pelt. So let's say you had 25 'rats and the fur buyer offered you $75 for the lot. You figured you could do better, so you took the pelts home and sent them off to Moyle's for tanning. Several months later, you get a bill from the tannery. It costs around $180 to tan and ship the pelts, so at this point you're into the fur for around $250 with the tanning cost and opportunity cost for not selling raw fur to the buyer. You also didn't get a fur check for the few months you were waiting. Now it's time to sell the 'rat pelts on Ebay and make some money.

Ebay is an online buying and selling platform that requires you to post up a listing of what you're looking to sell, including pictures, a description, shipping details, etc. You can figure on 10-15 minutes to put up a listing, which includes taking pictures, measuring the pelt, describing it in detail to potential buyers by writing a summary, estimating shipping cost and researching recent prices and sales of similar pelts, and deciding whether to sell via auction or fixed price. When you sell the item, you owe Ebay a sales commission, which is typically 10% of the sale price. There's also a Paypal commission for the transaction, which is around 3%. And remember, you can't just list all of your pelts at once and expect a good price, because you risk saturating the market and reducing buyer competition for each of your items.

Good quality tanned muskrat pelts typically sell on Ebay for around $15 apiece. With an opportunity cost of $3 and tanning cost of $7 and $1.50 commission, you theoretically stand to make an extra $3.50/pelt by selling tanned fur instead of selling it raw. If you don't mind the extra time and risk, this can be a decent way to get some added value for your fur, but many folks don't want to go through this process for just a couple of bucks. But if the fur buyer is offering you $1.50 average on 'rats, and they're selling for $20 each tanned on Ebay, the choice to sell tanned fur becomes a much easier one!

Higher price fur items offer greater risk, but greater opportunity for profit when sold as tanned fur. For instance, raw fur prices for good quality red fox have been averaging around $20 recently. With a tanning cost of about $25 and a total investment of about $50, display quality red fox can sell for around $80, for a potential profit of $30. There's also risk involved, because some are selling for a fair bit less than that.

In an open market like Ebay, it only takes one additional seller to flood a market and cause lower prices for a particular item. Remember that in times of low fur prices, other trappers will be tanning more of their fur as well, hoping to sell it in other avenues. There's no getting around a low market without being creative and standing out from the crowd with your product.

Etsy is another online selling platform (www.etsy.com) where you can set up a custom store to sell your goods. Similar to Ebay, you're at the mercy of supply and demand. Buyers on Etsy are usually looking for uniquely crafted items that they can't find in a regular marketplace, so creating outstanding products with your fur can potentially catch on and sell well there. If you're particularly creative, you could do well selling tanned fur items on Etsy.

Consigning tanned fur at local stores allows you to avoid the hassle of internet sales, but you will still have to give the store owner his or her cut, and it may take months or more to move the fur. If you live in a rural area that receives lots of tourist traffic, tanned fur sales can turn out to be quite profitable, and you often don't have to deal with competition flooding the market with low priced items. If you can, try to market your tanned fur as local, sustainably and legally harvested fur by a local trapper. That may catch the attention of buyers who are willing to pay extra for something they know is unique.

Sportsman's shows and craft fairs can be a good place to sell tanned fur. With so many potential buyers looking at your products, there's a great chance to make sales. Other platforms that command the attention of potential buyers can be good places to sell tanned fur as well, including Facebook and Instagram. It's important to have a large network of potential buyers on these platforms to convert sales.

Whether in local shops or online markets, selling tanned fur provides another alternative to consider when selling your fur. Just remember to pay attention to all of the details, time, effort and costs involved with this route, and factor those things into your decision-making during sale time. Oftentimes either sales method is a wash, but for some markets during some periods, choosing the right sales route can mean the difference between a nice profit and a discouraging loss.

Fur Garments

Finished garments are the end of the production line for wild fur. The fur market has always been structured such that economies of scale make it more profitable for trappers to sell raw fur as opposed to finished products. This fur is then tanned, processed, and made into coats, hats, gloves, scarves and other items in huge quantities at a low cost. Seldom does a trapper see caught fur all the way through to the sold garment stage, but that is an option that does exist today.

One option you have is to send your fur out to get tanned, and then craft your own items from the tanned fur. The things you can make with tanned fur are only limited by your imagination and, of course, your artistic and sewing/crafting ability. Years ago, I met a man ice fishing on a Maine lake wearing a muskrat fur hat he'd made himself. It looked incredibly comfortable and stylish at the same time, and I'm certain he could have sold as many of those hats as he could make, and at a profit to boot.

There are several online resources available to help instruct you on making clothing and decorative items with your tanned fur. Google, Youtube and an open mind are your friends when it comes to learning unique skills like making fur clothing.

If you're not so artistically inclined (like me), there's another option. Several companies will make a wide variety of creations out of your fur for a price. You can send them your tanned fur, pay to have items made (coats, hats, gloves, pillows, blankets, etc.), and sell those items through various outlets.

For instance, send them your tanned furs and Glacier Wear (www.glacierwear.com) will make you a mountain man hat for $55, a pair of 16" mittens for $100, ear muffs for $19, a fur pillow for around $75, and a number of other items. USA Foxx (www.usafoxx.com) provides similar services.

As far as selling your specialty fur items, be sure to have a good understanding of what you can sell them for and where you can sell them. Check out Fursource.com to see prices of items like fur pillows, ear muffs and other accessories. If you could sell items for similar prices to the Fur Source listings, it would be worth paying a company to tan your pelts, and paying another to make fur items out of them. However, remember that on a platform like Ebay you won't command the same high prices, and you may do better trying to make the items on your own.

Taxidermy Market

Taxidermists can sometimes be a great alternative to sell fur to, though usually only in small quantities. Depending on demand, local taxidermists may have a particular need for a certain animal. Oftentimes I'll check in with our taxidermists to see if they need a couple of the animals I'm catching. You never know what they need. A major outdoor retailer might be setting up a store and need a bunch of mounted furbearers for display. A customer might want a mounted mink, even though they don't trap.

If your taxidermist does happen to need an animal, it's often best to keep the whole animal frozen so they can prepare it the way they want. If you must skin it, follow taxidermist instructions on how to do so. Another great resource is the online taxidermy forums. I've successfully sold whole, frozen items at great prices to taxidermists online. Be sure to follow all applicable state laws regarding animal shipment across state lines. There are fast shipping services available, and good insulated packaging that make shipping frozen critters very feasible. Check out the wanted sections of the major taxidermy forums, like Taxidermy.net or Taxidermytalk.com.

THINKING OUTSIDE THE FUR: OTHER WAYS TO PROFIT FROM FURBEARERS

We've discussed the major avenues for selling fur, but realize that there are countless other ways to make money from furbearers. Use your imagination and try out new ideas. Some will work, others won't, but the only way to know for sure is to try.

Fly Tying – My Failed Experiment

A few years back, I wasn't happy with the prices I was getting for my raw fur, and decided to send most of my catch out to get tanned. While waiting for the furs to come back, I thought a lot about my options and researched a number of ideas. I was just getting into fly tying at the time, and noticed that some fly patterns called for the use of fur. After browsing a few fly shops, both local and online, I realized that many retailers were selling small patches of tanned fur for fly tyers, and at pretty good prices. After a little (but not enough) background research, I decided this would be an excellent business opportunity, and began to pursue it.

Before getting my fur back from the tannery, I purchased a bunch of tanned fur and fur scraps online, and started cutting up patches of fur and packaging it for sale in fly shops. I put together some attractive packaging and a business plan and started contacting shops. I had already invested a few hundred dollars and a lot of time in the idea when I began to realize I should have done a little more research on the business. It turns out those fur patches weren't really flying off the shelves. A kind fly tying supply distributor in Billings, Montana informed me that he only sold about 50 fur patches a year to the shops he supplied.

Five years later, I still had some inventory to sell from the failed business proposition. Part of me still wonders, though, if somehow the business could have worked. Though it was a failure, I'm not discouraged, and will continue to pursue fur selling alternatives in the future. You never know unless you try!

Meat Market

Many furbearers don't provide a quality eating experience, but raccoon and muskrat certainly do. In the southern United States, coon and 'rats are sold to individuals and restaurants for their meat. Folks love eating them, and during times of low fur prices, trappers often fetch more value from these critters for their meat than they do from selling the fur. Some people also like beaver meat, but no large commercial market for it currently exists.

The trapping bait industry is a good opportunity to sell meat from the furbearers you catch. Many formulated baits use beaver and muskrat meat as their base, and some use meat from other furbearers as well. You may have some success selling carcasses to bait and lure makers, or perhaps making your own.

Castor

If you're a beaver trapper and you aren't taking the castor from the beavers you skin, you're missing out on a lot. There is a large market for beaver castor because it is used in the making of perfumes and in food flavoring. It is also a very popular ingredient in many trapping lures, and purchased by lure makers. Pay attention to the fur auction results to stay on top of the beaver castor market. Price can fluctuate quite a bit and is directly related to market supply (number of beavers harvested). During years of high fur prices, beaver harvest is high and there is a lot of castor in the market, bringing prices down. The opposite is true during low fur price years, when beaver harvest is low and the castor market is hot. In recent years there have been some situations where the castor value was worth more than the pelt on a harvested beaver.

Miscellaneous Animal Parts

A number of other parts can be harvested from furbearers, and here's a place where you can get really creative. The best site I've found for markets of miscellaneous animal parts is Moscow Hide and Fur, at www.furbuyer.com. They buy skulls, claws and teeth from a number of furbearers. They list prices and conditions for each item on the site. This can be a great opportunity to get more value out of the furbearers you harvest. For instance, you can sell your bobcat skulls for $5 each, and sell the teeth for $0.25 apiece. Double that price for lynx. Coyote teeth sell for $0.25 each, and fox skulls at $3. They buy a ton of other items, so look over their list to see what you might have that is of value. The prices aren't extravagant, but every little bit counts. There are also other online forums and trapping supply companies that will buy these items from trappers.

Live Market
Hunting with dogs is a big industry in the southern United States, and there is a large demand for certain furbearer species to use in training dogs. If you can trap live animals like foxes and coyotes, and handle them properly, they sell for far more money than they would in the fur market.

Glands for the Lure Industry

Lure and urine are necessary supplies in the trapping business – every trapper needs them to effectively catch fur. The manufacture and sale of lure, urine and other specialty items is big business, and demand for scent glands and urine is high. If you are a high volume trapper who puts up your own fur, you can make decent money by saving the scent glands of the animals you process. Skunk essence extracted from the skunks you trap is extremely valuable as well. Lure makers pay good money for these items if you can get them in large quantities. Check with a lure maker or fur buyer near you for more information.

Conclusion

The fur market is a complex and ever-changing industry, but we as trappers don't have to feel powerless in the way we market our fur and the prices we accept. I hope this guide has provided you with a better understanding of the overall market, and helps you come up with strategies to market your fur more effectively. Regardless of market conditions, there will always be opportunity to profit for those who think with an open mind and adapt to the constantly changing market environment. Thanks for reading, and happy trapping!